GRAMMAR

For Beginners

Louise Anne Eveline Brunel

GRAMMAR For Beginners

© Louise Anne Eveline Brunel

Edited by Marie Ternel

National Library of Australia Cataloguing-in-Publication entry

Author:	Brunel, Louise Anne Eveline, author.
Title:	GRAMMAR For Beginners/ Louise Anne Eveline Brunel.
ISBN:	9780992439507 (paperback)
Subjects:	English language--Grammar--Juvenile literature
	English language--Grammar--Study and teaching (Primary) Grammar,
	Comparative and general--Juvenile literature. Language and languages--
	Grammars--Juvenile literature.
Dewey Number:	428.2

Published with the assistance of InHouse Publishing www.inhousepublishing.com.au

INTRODUCTION

The aim of this book is to help children better understand the use of English grammar.

I was a primary school teacher for over thirty-five years and know the need to encourage children to express themselves clearly and accurately.

Please use this book to assist in the understanding and use of English.

CONTENTS

LESSON ONE – WORDS

Grammar is the key to speaking and writing correctly. It is a combination of rules that should be followed. We use words to speak and write. Words consist of letters.

There are twenty-six letters: a, b, c, d, e, f, g, h, i, j, k, l, m, n, o, p, q, r, s, t, u, v, w, x, y, z. Together these form the alphabet.

The letters are divided into two categories, which are called consonants and vowels.

The consonants are: b, c, d, f, g, h, j, k, l, m, n, p, q, r, s, t, v, w, x, y, z.
The vowels are: a, e, i , o, u.

Words are made up of one, two, three or more syllables.

The word *man* has one syllable,
wo/man: has two syllables
beau/ti/ful: has three syllables
won/der/ful/ly: has four syllables

A combination of words with one or more verbs is called a **sentence**.
Example: She took her bag and went away.

A **phrase** is a combination of words *without* a verb.
Example: The long road with tall trees on each side.

Sentences and phrases form the basis of speech. There are nine parts of speech: **noun, article, adjective, pronoun, verb, adverb, preposition, conjunction and interjection**. Each of those is found in the following sentence:

Oh! The baby is fine and he is sitting quietly under that tree.
"Oh!" is an interjection,
"The" is an article,
"baby" is a noun,
"is" is a verb,
"fine" is an adjective,
"and" is a conjunction,
"he" is a pronoun,
"is sitting" is a verb,
"quietly" is an adverb,
"under" is a preposition,
"that" is an adjective and
"tree" is a noun.

LESSON 1 - REVISION AND TEST

1. In the following words, separate the vowels from the consonants: *daughter, visible, bookcase, bedroom, artificially, undertaken.*
    Example: daughter — d, g, h, t, r are the consonants; a, u, e are the vowels.

    _____

    _____

    _____

    _____

2. Separate the syllables in the words mentioned above.
    Example: daugh/ter — two syllables.

    _____

    _____

    _____

    _____

3. Name the different parts of speech contained in the following:
    (a) Look! We did run quickly but we were overtaken by them.

    _____

    _____

    _____

    _____

(b) My father works in a big factory not far from the blue lake.

_____

_____

_____

_____

_____

(c) They have bought a large house with a small garden.

_____

_____

_____

_____

_____

4. Write:
   1. Two sentences and underline the verb or verbs in each of them.

_____

_____

_____

_____

_____

(b) Two phrases.

_____

_____

_____

_____

LESSON TWO – PUNCTUATION

PUNCTUATION is essential when reading and writing. It is used to make the meaning of a sentence clearer. There are:

(a)   the **comma** (,) which means a brief pause.

(b)   the **full stop** (.) which is a complete pause or stop. It is placed at the end of a sentence.
        Examples: The man, his friend and a dog are walking along the road.
                        We were all running, jumping, trying hard to reach our destination.

(c)   the **semi-colon** (;) is normally used as a natural break, usually in a longer sentence.
        Example: He had played in the park with his friends all day and they had fun; it was
                        time to go home.

(d)   the **colon** (:) is used to introduce more information.
        Examples: I must tell you: the man never came as promised.
                        I was angry at the time: I didn't tell you then.

(e)   **inverted commas** (") or (') are used to indicate the spoken language
        Examples: My mother suddenly said, "John, go to your room now and start doing
                        your homework." He took his bag and replied, "I'll do that, Mum."

(f)   the **interrogation mark** (?) follows a question.
        Examples: "Where have you been?"
                        "Did you come to see me?"

(g)   the **exclamation mark** (!) is used to express emotion or give a command.
        Examples: "Oh! I was not far away."
                        "Yes, my dear, and what a beautiful dress you have on!"
                        "Look! Here they are!"

(h)   the **apostrophe** (') indicates possession.
        Examples: John's pen.
                        The boys' bikes.
            It can also be used to replace a missing letter or word:
        Examples: I'll go (I *will* go).
                        It's late (It *is* late).

(i)   the **hyphen** (-) is used to link two or more words.
        Examples: Twenty-four,
                        horse-drawn,
                        merry-go-round.

(j)   the **dash** (—) and

(k)   the **brackets** ( ) are used to indicate an extra comment.
       Examples: The bell rang — and yes, it was time to go home.
                       The baby was crying (as babies do).

LESSON 2 - REVISION AND TEST

1.   Read the following and apply the *punctuation*.

On the way home I met with a friend who asked me
Do you have anywhere to go tonight
        Why I asked him
        We could go to the city where there will be a big show we shall have nothing to
pay it is outside the building Even if there is no seat available we could sit on the lawn
and enjoy the show all the same Wont it be real fun What do you think of that such a
pleasure too to be together
        Great At what time are we leaving
        At seven o'clock we go to the railway station and buy our ticket then wait for the
train we should be at the venue by eight o'clock I think
        Thank you for inviting me what a nice time we shall have together I like music so
much Don't you

2.   Write a few sentences of your own using the different forms of *punctuation*.

_____

_____

_____

_____

_____

_____

_____

LESSON THREE - THE NOUN

The **NOUN** is used to denote a person, an animal or a thing.

> *Examples:*   brother, cat, chair.

There are two kinds of nouns: **common and proper**. The common noun denotes any person, animal or thing.

> *Examples:*   son, cow, car.

The proper noun is the name *particularly* given to a person, an animal or a thing.

> *Examples:*   *John* to a person;
>
> *Fido* to a dog;
>
> *Ford* to a car.

A *capital* letter is used for the first letter of a proper noun, as shown in the above examples.

EXERCISE:

1. In the following sentences underline each common noun with a single line and each proper noun with a double line.

    Peter is a fine boy; he has a Raleigh bike which he rides every day. His dog Blackie is always running after him.

2. Write down three common nouns and three proper nouns.

    _____

    _____

    _____

    _____

    _____

- ## THE GENDER

The **GENDER** is to distinguish between:

    (a) a *male* person or animal — **masculine**

    (b) a *female* person or animal — **feminine**

    (c) a *thing* — **neutral**

        Examples: man - horse *(masculine gender);*

                      woman — mare *(feminine gender);*

                      table, tree *(neutral gender)*

EXERCISE:

    1. State the gender of the following words:

              Aunt,

              Richard,

              cow,

              brother,

              flower,

              horse,

              lion,

              book,

              granddaughter,

              Mary,

              tigress.

    2. Write the feminine of each of the following:

Uncle (	*)*	*deer (*	*)*	*son (*	*)*
father (	*)*	*boy (*	*)*	*Lord (*	*)*
dog (	*)*	*master (*	*)*	*sir (*	*)*

    3. Write sentences containing:

(a) two words of *masculine* gender;

    Example: The man (masculine) and his son (masculine) are coming over

_____

_____

- _____

(b) one word of *feminine* gender;

  Example: The lady (feminine) was alone

_____

_____

_____

(c) two words of *neutral* gender;

  Example: She was carrying a bag (neutral) and an umbrella(neutral)

_____

_____

_____

4. Write a phrase containing:

  (a) one word of masculine gender;

  Example: The little boy happy at last,

_____

_____

_____

  (b) one word of feminine gender;

  Example: The cow grazing in the paddock

_____

_____

_____

  (c) two words of **neutral** gender.

  Example: The backpack over there near the door

_____

_____

_____

• THE NUMBER

The **NUMBER** is to determine the quantity of persons, animals or things. There are two types of numbers: the **singular,** which denotes *one* person, *one* animal or *one* thing, and the **plural,** which denotes *more than one* person, animal or thing.

> *Examples*:   A *girl* was picking a rose *(singular).*
>
>   The *boys* and their *friends* were all flying their *kites (plural).*

(a) A plural number is generally formed by adding an '**s**' to a singular noun: *girl/girls, cousin/cousins, pencil/pencils.*

(b) Nouns ending in *o, s, x, sh, ch* have '**es**' added: *hero/heroes, box/boxes, bus/buses, match/matches, church/churches.*

(c) An '**s**' is added to particular nouns ending in o: *piano/pianos, portfolio/portfolios.*

(d) For nouns ending in *f* or *fe,* change *f* or *fe* into '**v**' and add '**es**': *half/halves, thief/thieves, wife/wives.*

(e) For a few nouns ending in *f* or *fe,* no change is required, simply add '**s**': *proof/proofs, chief/chiefs, cliff/cliffs.*

(f) For nouns ending in *y;* change y into '**i**' and add '**es**': *fly/flies, pony/ponies.*

(g) For nouns ending in *ey* simply add '**s**': *key/keys, monkey/monkeys.*

(h) For the words man and woman change '**an**' into '**en**': *man/men, woman/women.*

(i) For some words, there is no change between plural and singular: series, sheep, salmon, scissors.

Exercise:

1. Write the following nouns in the plural form:

   The *donkey* (   ) and the *baby* (   )

   Both *bus* (   ) were full of *passenger* (   )

   Give me some *match* (   )

   Two *butterfly* (   ) were on these *flowerbed* (   )

   Those handkerchief (   ) are dirty

LESSON FOUR - THE ARTICLE

The **ARTICLE** is used to introduce a noun. There are two kinds of articles: **definite** and **indefinite**. The definite article '*the*' is used for a person, animal or thing already determined.

    Examples: The man; *the* dog; *the* tree.

The indefinite article '*a*' or '*an*' is not determined.

    Examples: A woman, a mouse, *a* flower: *any* woman, *any* mouse, *any* flower.

'*An*' is used before a noun starting with a vowel.

    Examples: An animal; *an* egg; *an* umbrella.

EXERCISE:

1. Write two *definite articles* in a sentence; underline them.

_____

_____

_____

2. Write two *indefinite articles* in two different sentences or phrases; underline them.

_____

_____

_____

LESSONS 3 AND 4 - REVISION AND TEST

This farmer has one son and two daughters. In his backyard there are several hens and a big rooster. There are also a few trees with beautiful flowers.

His wife cleans the house, takes the children to school in their big Holden car with the white hood. Mary, the elder sister, often plays with her brother Tom who is the youngest child. Younger sister Jane likes to ride Penny the grey mare seen grazing in the far back meadow.

They are a very close family:

1. Read the passage above and answer the following questions:

   (a) How many persons are there?

   _____

   (b) List the proper names mentioned. How are they related?

   _____

   _____

   _____

   (c) What are the mother's duties?

   _____

   (d) Can you name two flowering trees?

   _____

   _____

   _____

   (e) Where is the horse? Who is the rider?

   _____

   _____

   _____

(f) Who is Tom? With whom does he play?

_____

_____

_____

(g) Give a proper name to the father, the rooster, the wife, the meadow, the family, the school.

_____

_____

_____

(h) (i) Underline three sentences and (ii) number three phrases (1,2,3)

_____

_____

_____

(i) List the common nouns and the proper nouns.

_____

_____

_____

(j) Write separately the nouns of masculine gender, of feminine gender and of neutral gender?

Masculine

_____

Feminine

_____

Neutral

_____

2. Put in a singular form the following words: daughters, hens, horses, trees, knives, bushes, lilies, mangoes, foxes, daisies, donkeys, men, scarves.

_____

_____

_____

3. Put in a plural form the following: Brother, brush, rooster, key, dolly, handkerchief, meadow, family, chief, woman, domino, batch, garden, study, grotto.

_____

_____

_____

4. Fill in the blanks with the appropriate article:

Bob (   ) little boy had (   ) apple in one hand
and (   ) cake in the other.
(   ) hunter has seen (   ) eagle on top of the
tree in (   ) forest nearby. He has (   ) eye on (   ) bird
and (   ) gun ready to shoot at it.

LESSON FIVE - THE ADJECTIVE

- ## QUALITATIVE

All the words below in italics are **qualitative adjectives**; they denote the quality of persons, animals and things.

Examples: The *old* man has a *black* dog and a *white* cat.

My mother is a *kind* and *generous* woman.

This tree has *green* leaves and *yellow* flowers.

EXERCISE:

1. In the following sentences look for the qualitative adjectives and underline them.
   The big cat has caught a little mouse.

   The new butcher uses a long knife with a sharp blade.

   His sister has fair hair and blue eyes.

2. Write three sentences of your own and underline the qualitative adjectives.

_____

_____

_____

_____

_____

- ## COMPARATIVE

Note the **comparative adjectives** in italics used in the sentences below: the quality of the persons, animals or things is being compared.

Examples: This cake is *sweet*, mine is *sweeter*, but the other one on the table is the *sweetest*.

My rope is *longer* than John's, yours is the *longest*.

This cow is *big*, the other one is *bigger* and the third in the far away meadow is the *biggest*.

My sister is *tall*, my brother is *taller*, but our cousin is the *tallest*.

(a) To compare two persons, animals or things add 'er' to the adjective. To compare more than two, add 'est'.

(b) In some cases, the last consonant is doubled before an 'er' or 'est' is added, as in big; bigger; biggest.

(c) When an adjective has more than *two syllables,* use '**more**' and '**most**',

      Examples: (i) beautiful; **more** beautiful; **most** beautiful

                  (ii) This is an exciting story, I have read a **more** exciting one, but Cinderella is the **most** exciting one.

(d) When an adjective ends in y change y into 'i' and add 'er' and 'est', as in pretty; prett**ier**; prett**iest**.

EXERCISE:

Give an example of a comparative adjective.

_____

_____

_____

• INDEFINITE

The words in italics in the following examples are **indefinite adjectives:** They are not precise or exact.

      Examples: I have *many* friends. *All* the boys are brave.

                 Some fruits are excellent, *other* ones are not so.

                 Few people were present but there were *several* cars.

                 Neither a boy *nor a* girl was present.

EXERCISE:

Use: *many, some, several, neither, nor,* in sentences of your own.

_____

_____

_____

_____

_____

• NUMERAL CARDINAL

The words in italics in the following are **numeral cardinal adjectives**. They are used when counting

> *Examples:*   I have *two* pens and *three* pencils.
>
> He has a *hundred* cows.
>
> More than a *thousand bees* are in this hive.

• NUMERAL ORDINAL

The words in italics in the following are **numeral ordinal adjectives**. They indicate order or rank.

> *Examples:*   He is in the *fifth* class.
>
> The *tenth* car is mine.
>
> I'll come to see you on the *sixteenth* of this month.
>
> He is the *hundredth* soldier of the regiment.

EXERCISE:

Fill in the blanks with suitable numeral adjectives.

In the basket, there are (   ) mangoes and (   ) peaches.

You are the (   ) boy standing in that line.

They are going to the (   ) shop to buy (   ) cakes.

Put my (   ) books on the (   ) shelf, please.

This is the (   ) bird flying to that tree.

The dog has (   ) good legs, the (   ) is broken.

• POSSESSIVE

My, his, her, its, your, our, their– are **possessive adjectives**. They denote ownership.

> *Examples:*   *My* pen is lost.
>
> *His* mother is in the bedroom.
>
> *Your* hands are clean.
>
> *Her* father is at work.
>
> The poor animal has broken one of *its* legs.
>
> *Our* garden is fine.
>
> The pupils have gone to *their* school.

EXERCISE:

    1.   Use three possessive adjectives in sentences of your own

_____

_____

_____

_____

    2.   Fill in the blanks with suitable possessive adjectives.

The two friends have lost (   ) way in the bush.

Where have you put (   ) bag?

We have put (   ) money together to buy the car.

The school is not very far. We can see (   ) grounds from here.

I can't find (   ) ruler.

My sister is carrying (   ) own suitcase.

• DEMONSTRATIVE

An adjective written before a noun and referring to a particular person or thing is a demonstrative adjective. *This, that, these, those* when written before a noun or another adjective are **demonstrative adjectives**.

Examples: *This* book is full of good stories.

                That boy has gone to meet his friend.

                Put *these* flowers in that vase.

                You have eaten all *those* apples.

EXERCISE:

Use demonstrative adjectives in sentences of your own.

_____

_____

_____

_____

_____

• SYNONYMS

All the words in italics in the following examples have the same meaning: they are **synonyms**.

Examples: A *large* stone — A *big* rock.

A *high* wall — A *tall* tree.

My *little* sister with her *small* bag.

Dark sky — *Black* clouds.

Good girl — *Nice* boy.

EXERCISE:

Write a synonym for each word in italics:

This girl is *beautiful* (   ).

The dog is *sick* (   ).

She was *happy* (   ).

He was *seen* (   ) in the *woods* (   ).

Several (   ) people were *assembled* (   ) *close to* (   ) the shop.

There were *a few* (   ) coins in my purse; he *stole* (   ) them.

• ANTONYMS

Each word in italics in the following examples is the **antonym (opposite or contrary)** of the other:

Examples: He is a *good* and *brave* boy. He is a *naughty* and *cowardly* boy.

They have *new* books to *buy*. They have *old* books to *sell*.

EXERCISE:

Fill in each blank with the antonym of the word in italics.

Empty (   ) the bottle; put it *down* (   ) here.

The *big* (   ) dog is *standing* (   ) *next to* (   ) the *tall* (   ) tree.

The kitten is a *male* (   ).

Something (   ) could be done *fortunately* (   ).

This street is very *quiet* (   ).

I have put the vase *on* (   ) the *large* (   ) table.

LESSON 5 - REVISION AND TEST

Fill in each blank with a suitable adjective:

She has a (   ) dress and a (   ) hat.

(   ) dog has (   ) broken leg.

There are (   ) birds on (   ) (   ) tree.

The mango is the (   ) fruit for me.

He showed me (   ) pictures.

My backyard is (   ) than yours.

The holidays will start on the (   ) of June.

(   ) garden is full of the (   ) beautiful flowers.

My friend Tom has (   ) name on (   ) (   ) book.

Mary had (   ) photo taken not long ago.

There are only (   ) shops round the corner of (   ) street.

LESSON SIX - THE PRONOUN

The **PRONOUN** is the word used to replace a noun.

• PERSONAL

I, me, you, he, she, it, they, them, us, myself, yourself, himself, herself, itself, ourselves, yourselves, themselves are personal pronouns:

Examples:	My father is tidying the garage — *he* is tidying it.
	Your sister is a nice person-*she* is really nice.
	John and Andrew are my good friends — *they* are my good friends. *I* like *them*.
	The boys were standing in the yard, *they* were singing.
	The fruits are in the small basket, bring *them* to *me*.
	Why are *you* standing there?
	I'm coming to join *you*.
	Come with *me*, let *us* go to the shop together.
	My brother and *I*, *we* are in the same class.
	I did the work *myself*.
	He is asking something for *himself*.
	My sister has gone to the shop by *herself*.
	John! Do *it yourself*, please.
	Peter and Mary! *You yourselves* are responsible for everything.
	They were really enjoying *themselves*.

• RELATIVE

A **relative pronoun** relates to a person, animal or objects already mentioned. The words in italics in the examples below are all relative pronouns.

Examples:	The beggar *who* is sitting in front of the shops is old.
	The woman *whom* you were talking to is my sister.
	I have seen the horse *which* was grazing there.
	This lesson is *what* I told you about.
	The ring *that* your friend lost yesterday has been found.
	The books *that* are on the table are full of pictures.

EXERCISE:

Fill in each blank with either a personal or a relative pronoun, whichever is applicable:

Let (   ) go and pick up the fruits (   ) the wind has blown down. (   ) really like (   ).

Have (   ) taken the pen (   ) was on the table?

(   ) was talking to the woman (   ) met the day before.

Bring back to (   ) the book (   ) lent (   ) yesterday.

The lady (   ) is sitting there on the beach is a friend (   ) I have not seen for a long time.

Tell (   ) what (   ) want from (   ).

• POSSESSIVE

Mine, ours, yours, his, hers, theirs are **possessive pronouns**. They denote ownership.

Examples: Those books are *mine.*

Bumper, the small dog, is *his.*

Are all those cakes *hers?* No, they are *yours,* I bought them for you.

These pencils are all *theirs* not *ours.*

The word *his* can be either a possessive pronoun or a possessive adjective. It is an adjective if placed before a noun.

Example: Referring to my friend's cat - The cat is *his* (pronoun)

His (adjective) cat likes to play with me.

EXERCISE:

Use each of the *possessive* pronouns mentioned above in a sentence of your own.

_____

_____

_____

_____

_____

• DEMONSTRATIVE

This, that, these, those are **demonstrative pronouns.**

> Examples: *This* is my coat, I left it here yesterday.
>
> *That* doesn't belong to you.
>
> Take *these* for you, John.
>
> *Those* are ripe ones.

This, that, these, those are **demonstrative adjectives** when they are placed before a noun or another adjective.

> Examples: *This* coat is mine, I left it here yesterday.
>
> *That* house belongs to him.
>
> Take *these ripe* fruits for you, John.
>
> *Those* fruits over there should be thrown out.

EXERCISE:

Write examples of your own.

_____

_____

_____

• INDEFINITE

All the words in italics in the examples below are **indefinite pronouns.** They are not specific.

> Examples: *All* the fruits are over there. *None* are for you.
>
> *Several* are still unripe. Throw away *some* of them. Keep *some* for the birds.
>
> I have already kept a *few*. *Others* should definitely be thrown out.
>
> *Neither* of the boys should eat them.
>
> Make sure *nobody* else eats them.

• INTERROGATIVE

The words in italics in the examples below are **interrogative pronouns.** They ask a question:

> Examples: *What* do you have to say? *Who* is that man standing there?
>
> For *whom* are you waiting? *Which* of the two do you want?

Whose and *which* in the following sentences are **interrogative adjectives.** They are placed before a noun.

> Examples: Whose book is this? Which house are you looking for?

LESSON 6 - REVISION AND TEST

1.   Fill in each blank with a suitable pronoun:

The boys (   ) were there went away; (   ) were going to meet (   ).

Do (   ) like your school, Peter?

(   ) is what (   ) likes best.

Those books are (   ), I (   ) find them quite interesting.

She did the work by (   ); (   ) helped (   ).

(   ) of these boys went to the match?

(   ) was quite satisfied with the play.

2.   Write sentences of your own with:

(a)   a relative pronoun;

_____

_____

_____

(b)   a demonstrative pronoun;

_____

_____

_____

(c) a personal pronoun;

_____

_____

_____

(d) an indefinite pronoun;

_____

_____

_____

(e) a possessive pronoun.

_____

_____

_____

3.   In the following sentences state whether each word in italics is an adjective or a pronoun.

   Example: He (personal pronoun) has lost *his* (possessive adjective) pen in *this* (demonstrative adjective) street.

That (   ) is what I (   ) want, *you*(   ) know.

The lady *whom* (   ) you (   ) are talking about is sick.

Take care of *my* (   ) cat, please.

Their (   ) father has gone to town.

Which (   ) story are *you* (   ) telling *them* (   )?

They (   ) are talking about the woman *whose* (   ) dog is lost in

that (   ) forest.

All (   ) *those* (   ) fruits are *theirs* (   ).

These (   ) are all *mine* (   ).

To *whom* (   ) is *she* (   ) talking?

This (   ) is your bag, don't take *his* (   ).

Have *you* (   ) seen *her* (   ) mother?

She (   ) is a fine woman.

Which (   ) will you have?

Nobody (   ) likes *him* (   ).

LESSON SEVEN - THE VERB

VERB MEANS ACTION

Read, stand, run are **VERBS**. Action of reading, action of standing, action of running. The key action words are doing, being or being done.

> *Examples:*   I kicked the ball (doing the action).
>
> It was kicked back to me (action being done). It was mine (being).
>
> The horse will run the race (doing the action).
>
> Question: Who kicked the ball? Answer: *I.*
>
> Question: What was kicked back? Answer: *it.*
>
> Question: What was mine? Answer: *it.*
>
> Question: What will run the race? Answer: *horse.*

The words *I, it, horse* which answer the questions: *who* for persons; *what* for animals and things, are called the *subject* of the verb. So, the subject does the action, or has the action done to it.

> **EXERCISE:**
>
> Underline the subject with a single line and the verb with a double line in the following sentences:
>
> > The children are standing in the classroom.
> > You will take a rest, says the teacher.
> > The movie was shown to us. We enjoyed it.

• TRANSITIVE

A **transitive verb** is a verb that has a **direct object**.

> *Examples:*   I *like* this fruit.
>
> Question: What do I like? Answer: this fruit.
>
> They *take* the children to school.
>
> Question: Whom do they take? Answer: the children.
>
> You *feed* the cat every morning.
>
> Question: What do you feed? Answer: the cat.
>
> *Fruit, children, cat* are direct objects of the verbs *like, take, feed.*

Transitive verbs can also have one or more **indirect objects**.

> *Examples:*   They take the children to *school.*
>
> Question: Where do they take the children?
>
> Answer: to school.
>
> You feed the cat every *morning.*
>
> Question: When do you feed the cat?
>
> Answer: every morning.
>
> *School, morning,* are indirect objects of the verbs *take, feed.*

EXERCISE:

Underline the verb with a single line, the direct object with a double line and the indirect object with a triple line in the following:

The butcher sells meat to people

I bought some vegetables at the market.

We saw a big black cat on the road.

- ## INTRANSITIVE

Intransitive verbs have no direct objects.

Examples: The baby *is sleeping* in his cot.

They *stood* alone in the yard.

The sun *rises* every morning.

It *sets* at night.

The verbs — *is sleeping, stood, rises, sets* — are intransitive verbs. They *do not* have a direct object when the questions *whom* or *what* are put to them. They only have indirect objects, which are *cot, yard, morning, night.*

EXERCISE:

Write two sentences using intransitive verbs and underline the indirect objects.

_____

_____

_____

_____

LESSON 7 - REVISION AND TEST

In the following sentences underline the subject, the direct object and the indirect object.

Example: We (subject) took the car (direct object) and drove away through the park (indirect object).

Mother sent me to the shop where I bought food for the cat.

Nobody has taken the ball to the school.

You have two kittens and a goat in your back yard.

My sister drives me to school every day.

• Tenses

The tense indicates when the action takes place:

Examples: We learn English every day. (**Present Tense**)

We are learning English now. (**Present Continuous Tense**)

We have learned English already. (**Present Perfect (completed) Tense**)

We learned English yesterday. (**Past Tense**)

We were learning English at the time. (**Past Continuous Tense**)

We had learned English. (**Past Perfect Tense**)

We will learn English tomorrow. (**Future Tense**)

We will be learning English soon. (**Future Continuous Tense**)

We will have learned English by then. (**Future Perfect Tense**)

EXERCISE:

1.   Write in the brackets the tense of each verb used in the following sentences. Underline each verb.

Example: The children always <u>take</u> a trip to the football ground. (Present Tense)

My brother goes to school late very often. (   )

They all went to the farm last night. (   )

I have been to the market twice. (   )

Mother is cooking dinner. (   )

They will have breakfast soon. (   )

The baby was sitting on his small chair. (   )

I called you twice this morning. (   )

2.   Write sentences using the verbs

(a)   *get, make, stand* (i) in the present tense (ii) in the present continuous tense.

_____

_____

_____

(b)   *bring, follow, think* (i) in the past tense (ii) past continuous tense.

_____

_____

_____

(c)   *take, open, walk* in the future tense.

_____

_____

_____

3.   Write two sentences similar to the following examples:
     If you *are* late, you *will* stay home.

_____

_____

_____

     If you *were* late, you *would* stay home.

_____

_____

_____

4.   Write two sentences similar to the following examples, using the word *since*.
     We have made great progress *since* you were here.

_____

_____

_____

     The house *has changed since* you came.

_____

_____

_____

A verb can change to suit its subject.

Examples: I sit
He/she/it sits
We/they sit

I go
He/she/it goes
We/they go

LESSON EIGHT - THE ADVERB

An **ADVERB** is a word used to add to the meaning of a verb, an adjective or another adverb.

(a) The words in italics in the following examples are adverbs. They are answers to the question — *How*?

He ran (verb) *quickly* to catch the train

— *How* did he run? *Quickly*

--The creek is *completely* dry (adjective)

How dry is the creek? *Completely*

He writes *very neatly* (adverb)

How neatly does he write? *very*

EXERCISE:

Write three sentences using the 'how' question

_____

_____

_____

_____

(b) The words in italics in the following examples are adverbs. They are answers to the question — *When*?

He did all the work *yesterday*

— *When* did he do the work? *Yesterday*

She will do the gardening *tomorrow*

— *When* will she do the gardening? *Tomorrow*

My father will come *soon*

— *When* will my father come? *Soon*

EXERCISE:

Write three sentences using the "when" question

_____

_____

_____

_____

(c) The words in italics are adverbs. They are answers to the question – *How often*?

She does the shopping *every day*

— *How* often does she do the shopping? *Every day*

Mother goes to the gym weekly

— *How* often does mother go to the gym? *Weekly*

My sister is *always* late for school

— *How* often is my sister late for school? *Always*

EXERCISE:

Write three sentences using the "How Often" question

_____

_____

_____

_____

(d) The words in italics are adverbs. They are answers to the question — *Where?*

I went *there* to meet him

— *Where* did you go to meet him? *There*

Put all the books *here*

— *Where* do you put the books? *Here*

She has seen the dog *somewhere* on the beach

— *Where* has she seen the dog? *Somewhere*

I am going *nowhere*

— *Where* am I going? *Nowhere*

EXERCISE:

Write three sentences using the 'where' question

_____

_____

_____

_____

Adverbs are sometimes formed from adjectives.

Example: Gentle — *gently*, joyful — *joyfully*; merry — *merrily*:

EXERCISE:

Find four other adjectives and change them into adverbs.

_____

_____

_____

_____

LESSON 8 - REVISION AND TEST

Fill in the blanks with suitable adverbs.

All the boys will play football (　　　　　　　　)

They (　　　　　　　　) ride their bicycle.

They have not finished (　　　　　　　　)

They (　　　　　　　　) have one mile to ride.

Is the man (　　　　　　　　) late for work?

Don't talk (　　　　　　　　) please.

Mother takes us to school (　　　　　　　　)

She (　　　　　　　　) buys cakes for us.

The dress was (　　　　　　　　) made.

We walked (　　　　　　　　) because we were late.

She went (　　　　　　　　) into town.

Are you going (　　　　　　　　) tonight?

LESSON NINE - THE PREPOSITION

The **PREPOSITION** is another part of speech. It links a noun/pronoun to another word. All the words in italics in the following examples are prepositions.

> *Examples:*   There are many beautiful flowers *in* this garden.
>
>   They are walking *along* the road.
>
>   Put the box *on* the table.
>
>   We all went *to* town.
>
>   The girls are talking *among* themselves.
>
>   The train is travelling *under* the tunnel.
>
>   The athletes are running *towards* the finish line.

EXERCISE:

1.   Fill in each blank with a preposition.

Two birds are flying (   ) the branches. There is a nest (   ) that tree with two small birds (   ) it.

Let us talk (   ) our team.

We were walking (   ) the bushes where we met an old man taking his dog (   ) the veterinarian.

2.   Write three sentences each containing one or two prepositions.

_____

_____

_____

_____

LESSON TEN - THE CONJUNCTION

The **CONJUNCTION** is a word used to link two words, two phrases or two sentences. The words in italics in the following examples are conjunctions.

Examples: Mary *and* John are coming to see you *and* you can all have a good time.

They like to play music *or* to dance.

They will have *either* a cake or a piece of fruit.

This small village is situated *between* the country *and* the city.

Nobody *but* you *and* me.

Nothing to do *but* to sit down.

EXERCISE:

Choose three of the above conjunctions and use them in sentences of your own.

_____

_____

_____

_____

LESSON ELEVEN – THE INTERJECTION

All the words in italics are **INTERJECTIONS**. They are used to express an emotion or give a command. They are always followed by an exclamation mark (!).

Examples: *Oh!* What a beautiful day.

Eh! you, come here.

Stop! Hold on!

Hear! Hear!

Hey! Stop fooling yourself!

Hullo! Are you there?

EXERCISE:

Choose two interjections and use them in sentences of your own.

_____

_____

_____

_____

GENERAL REVISION – READING LESSONS

• SPRING

After the cold and harsh months of winter, we all welcome spring. Spring brings with its presence, a mild sun in a blue sky. At dawn, it's still slightly cold after a warm night. Plants start budding and flowers will soon appear. Birds start chirping again. There is a light wind. We can see children in the open flying their kites. Everybody looks happy.

REVISION AND TEST

1. Look for all the qualitative adjectives in the Reading Lesson and write them down.

   _____

   _____

   _____

   _____

2. Form an adverb from each of the following:

   harsh (   ) mild (   ) warm (   )
   light (   ) open (   ) happy (   )

3. Give the opposite (antonym) of:

   harsh (   ) mild (   ) warm (   )
   light (   ) open (   ) happy (   )
   presence (   ) night (   )
   appear (   ) can (   )
   everybody (   ) start (   )

4. Turn to the Reading Lesson and answer the questions:

1. Can you name the spring months?

   _____

2. Spring is a season. Can you name another season?

   _____

3. How many seasons are there in all?

   _____

   Choose one of them and write a sentence describing it.

   _____

   _____

   _____

4. Can you name two flowers?

   _____

5. What could the children do, apart from flying their kites?

   _____

   _____

   _____

5. Write each of the following sentences

      I watch television.

      They all bring their own kite and fly it.

      We start to play.

(a) in the past tense,

_____

_____

_____

(b) in the present perfect tense,

_____

_____

_____

(c) in the future tense,

_____

_____

_____

6. Give the comparative adjective for the following:

warm, light; happy, using them in short sentences.

Example: Cold, colder, coldest.

              Spring is cold, autumn is colder, winter is the coldest.

_____

_____

_____

• THE RIVER

A river generally flows from a source at the foot of a mountain or hill. This source has been formed by the accumulation of rain water which has found its way through cracks in the rocks. This water is trapped underground for a very, long time.

Then, one day, it suddenly gushes out. A spring is formed which starts flowing down as a stream. The land on which it flows is called the riverbed.

During its course, the river may meet with other streams. These streams are called tributaries and where they meet is called the confluence. The river then starts getting wider and wider and if it comes to a cliff it drops steeply and forms a waterfall.

The river continues its course till it comes to a lake or the sea, into which it discharges its waters. That part of the river is called the mouth of the river or the estuary.

REVISION AND TEST

1.   Read the above passage and answer the questions:

(a)   What is a source?

_____

_____

_____

(b)   Where is it formed?

_____

_____

_____

(c)   Can you think of a reason for the water to be trapped underground?

_____

_____

_____

(d)   What part is called the riverbed?

_____

_____

_____

(e)   What is a tributary?

_____

_____

_____

(f)   Where does a river last discharge its waters?

_____

_____

_____

2.   Write in the plural form:

A river begins. This source has been formed a year ago. It flows as a stream. When it comes to a cliff it tumbles down. This is a waterfall. The river may meet with another stream. This stream is called a tributary. The river continues its course till it reaches a lake.

_____

_____

_____

_____

3. State the tense of each of the following verbs:

It begins (   )

The source has been formed (   )

It is entering the sea (   )

It will meet with tributaries (   )

They had been formed (   )

4. Write down all the prepositions found in the Reading Lesson.

_____

_____

_____

_____

_____

5. Write three sentences, each containing an interjection.

_____

_____

_____

_____

_____

_____

6. Complete these sentences:

(a) If I went to the river, I (   )

(b) If you are there (   )

(c) The river flows into (   )

(d) Where the land is steep (   )

(e) The river will overflow if it (   )

• THE SPIDER (PART 1)

One day, I was walking along the bank of a stream which flows by my father's property. I sat down on a big flat rock for a rest. The water was running with a gentle murmur.

There were many trees on each side of the stream . I noticed a large spider crawling towards the end of a branch where it stayed quietly for some time. Then I saw it hanging from that branch on some kind of thread. As the spider advanced slowly, the thread became longer and longer till the spider reached another branch on the other side of the stream. It stayed there for a while. The spider then started working on the thread going round and round, downwards, upwards, many, many times. It was weaving its web with great skill. When the web was finished, I thought it was the best lace I had ever seen. (To be continued)

REVISION AND TEST

1. Answer the questions:

    1. Where was the stream?

        _____

    2. Was the stream silent? Explain your answer.

        _____

        _____

    3. How many sides does a river have?

        _____

    4. Where was the spider at first?

        _____

    5. How did it start its web?

        _____

    6. To what was this web compared?

        _____

2. Give another word (synonym) for each of the following:

large (   ) rock (   )

gentle murmur (   ) stream (   )

kind (   ) finish (   )

weave(   ) reach (   )

3. Choose three of the above words and write them in sentences of your own.

_____

_____

_____

4. Put in a plural form:

I was walking.

_____

She is writing.

_____

He stands still.

_____

It is a big insect.

_____

There is a tall tree.

_____

The spider was weaving a fine web.

_____

One stream was flowing.

_____

I became interested.

_____

It was building its nest.

_____

My brother is reading his book.

_____

5.   Fill in each blank with a possessive adjective:

   She likes (   ) father's property.

   The river follows (   ) course.

   I walked around (   ) property.

   Do you understand (   ) work?

   Let us take (   ) time to watch the spider.

   My uncle and my aunt are walking along with (   ) dog.

• THE SPIDER (PART 2)

The spider had chosen a good spot to set up its web. The web would be a fine trap. There were all kinds of insects flying around. The spider knew that some of these insects would be caught in the sticky string of which the web had been made. They would be good food.

After completing the web, the spider stayed in a corner — some kind of hiding place — not very far and kept watching.

Suddenly an insect was caught in the web. The spider quickly approached it. Taking it away, it started dissecting it before eating it.

Once or twice, big insects were caught in the web. While struggling to get away, they ruined it. The spider came up and very patiently repaired the damage, then went back to its watching place.

"Very clever," I said to myself. I couldn't help admiring the skill and courage of that spider. As I had been sitting there for a long time, I decided it was time to go back home.

REVISION AND TEST

1. Answer the questions:

    (a) Why was the spot chosen, a good one?

    _____

    (b) What was the web made of?

    _____

    (c) What was good food for the spider?

    _____

    (d) What did the spider do with the insect it trapped?

    _____

    (e) How was the web ruined?

    _____

    (f) Name three insects.

    _____

2.   All kinds of insects *were flying* around.

   The above sentence uses the verb *to fly* in the past continuous tense.

   Write down other sentences with the verb *to fly* in the following tenses:

(a)   the present continuous;

_____

_____

_____

(b)   the past tense;

_____

_____

_____

(c)   the present perfect;

_____

_____

_____

(d)   the future tense.

_____

_____

_____

3.   Choose three adverbs from the Reading Lesson and use them in sentences of your own.

_____

_____

4. Good spot: *Good* is a qualitative adjective. Find three others and use each before a noun.

_____

_____

_____

_____

_____

5. Fill in the blanks with a personal pronoun:

(   ) will be found near the river.

(   ) always walk together to the stream

(   ) and I (   ) like to walk around our property.

(   ) never walks alone, my sister accompanies (   ).

Keep waiting, (   ) will soon arrive:

(   ) can tell you.

6. Write down the first paragraph of the Reading Lesson.

Underline (a) the subjects with a single line and (b) the direct objects with a double line.

Example: The <u>spider</u> had chosen a good <u>spot</u>.

_____

_____

_____

_____

_____

_____

• JACK AND TOM

Jack and his brother Tom were returning home from school. As rain was falling heavily, Tom said to Jack, "Let us go under that tree and take cover for a while."

So, both stood under the big tree on the side of the road. After a while, Jack said, "Tom, let us keep walking, Mother might be worried if we are late."

"You are right, Jack, let us run then."

They started running. Suddenly a fierce flash of lightning lit up the sky and a thundering noise followed.

Looking back, Jack and Tom saw that the lightning had struck the big tree which they had just left, breaking off a large branch.

They realised that, if they had still been standing there, they too would have been struck by the lightning and probably been hurt.

"Thank God! We left the sheltering spot in time," said Jack.

Never stand under any tree during a storm. It's too dangerous.

REVISION AND TEST

1. Answer the questions:

    (a) What were the boys doing on the road?

    _____

    (b) Which of them had the idea of sheltering under the tree?

    _____

    (c) Why didn't they stand for long under the tree?

    _____

    (d) What happened to the tree?

    _____

    (e) What did the boys conclude?

    _____

2.	What kind of nouns are Jack and Tom?

_____

Write two other proper nouns of (a) girls (b) animals (c) places.

_____

_____

3.	Note the following tenses:

Present	Present Continuous
returns	*is returning*
Past	Present Perfect
returned	*has or have returned*

Apply the same tenses to the following verbs:

fall	_____

say	_____

stand	_____

run	_____

cover	_____

strike	_____

4.	Choose from the Reading Lesson six different prepositions and write them down.

_____

_____

_____

_____

5. Write (a) two sentences (b) two phrases of your own.

_____

_____

_____

_____

6. Write the appropriate pronoun in each blank:

Tom and Jack: (   ) were returning from school.

The lightning: (   ) was quite visible.

Tom and Jack: (   ) took shelter under a tree;

(   ) took every precaution.

(   ) was there when the lightning struck.

Take (the boy) (   ) to the shelter.

• GRANDMA'S BALCONY (PART 1)

There were all kinds of green plants growing in pots on Grandma's balcony. As these pots were very close together, the leaves of some of the plants became entangled, making the balcony look like a miniature forest.

One day, a turtledove, probably looking for a place to lay its eggs, noticed the balcony and bravely chose a space between the ferns for its nest. It quietly settled down.

Some time later, Grandma found that there were two whitish eggs in the nest.

The turtledove was not afraid of Grandma. She could go on the balcony any time she wanted.

The bird sat on the eggs. Every now and then, it flew away, but always came back to brood.

After a few days, there were two small, featherless and ugly birds in the nest. They were waiting for their mother. It kept flying back and forth bringing food in her beak for them.

The young birds started growing their feathers little by little, till they became beautiful fully grown birds. However, they were still not strong enough to leave the nest.

One day, while Grandma was on the balcony, the birds rose from the nest, looked straight at her as if to say: "thank you for the hospitality", then flew away. (To be continued)

REVISION AND TEST

1. Answer the questions:

   (a) What kind of plants were on Grandma's balcony?

   _____

   (b) Why did the turtledove choose the balcony?

   _____

   (c) What colour were the eggs?

   _____

   (d) Why did the bird sit on the eggs?

   _____

   (e) Name one thing mother bird could have taken to her little ones to eat?

   _____

(f) Did the birds stay in the nest when they were grown up?
Explain your answer.

_____

_____

2. From the second paragraph of the Reading Lesson, choose (a) five words of one syllable; (b) four words of two syllables; (c) two words of three syllables.

_____

_____

_____

3. Put in the singular form:
All kinds of plants; some leaves; there were two white eggs; the ferns on the balconies; few days have passed; two small birds; they were turtledoves.

_____

_____

_____

4. Use the words (a) '*a*'; (b) 'an' before three different words.

_____

_____

_____

5. Beautiful is an adjective: Write down four other adjectives from the Reading Lesson above.

_____

6. Form a noun from: beautiful, strong, ugly, sad, choose, long, pretty, good, brave.

_____

_____

_____

7. Write sentences using who, which, what as *interrogative pronouns*.

_____

_____

_____

_____

_____

• GRANDMA'S BALCONY (PART 2)

Some time later came another turtledove, or it may have been the same one. All these birds look alike: grey feathers with a spot of white here and there.

The turtledove did the same thing, settled in the same nest, then laid two eggs which also produced two small, ugly, featherless, birds.

But, this time, something went wrong. For some unknown reason, the mother -bird never came back. The small birds were left alone in the nest and unfortunately died, probably of starvation.

This was very sad indeed, but it wasn't all. When Grandma put her hand in the nest to remove the dead birds, her hand was covered with lice. There were lice everywhere. Poor Grandma, she had to disinfect the balcony.

From then on, she had to scare off any bird which approached the balcony.

She learned a lesson: 'Never to allow any bird to nest on her balcony'.

REVISION AND TEST

1. Answer the questions:

   (a) From the above passage, how would you describe a turtledove.

   _____

   (b) Write down the names of two other birds. State their colours.

   _____

   (c) What happened to those little birds? Explain why.

   _____

   (d) What happened to Grandma's balcony?

   _____

   (e) What are lice? Put lice in the singular form.

   _____

2. *This, that, these, those* are either adjectives or pronouns.

    In the following sentences state whether they are adjectives or pronouns.

    That mother-bird did not come back. (   )

    This was very sad indeed. (   )

    All *those* birds are the same (   )

    That is Grandma's balcony (   )

    This time, it was not the same (   )

    Let *these* plants grow (   )

    Those were not big enough (   )

    These are particular birds (   )

3. Write the opposite (antonym) of each of the following:

    beautiful (   ); white (   ); something (   );

    wrong (   ); small (   ); never (   );

    came (   ); sad (   ); covered (   );

    poor (   ); dead (   ).

4. Fill each blank with a subject.

    (   ) builds its nest.

    (   ) all went to the balcony.

    (   ) died of starvation.

    (   ) of the two birds stayed?

    (   ) will stay with us.

    (   ) was all by myself.

    When (   ) comes back (   ) will give you something to eat.

    (   ) likes those insects.

5. Fill in the blanks with *myself, himself, themselves, ourselves, herself, yourself, yourselves, itself.*

    Children, you have but (   ) to blame.

    The bird built its nest by (   ).

    My friends and I, we (   ) completed the whole work.

    You did the writing (   ).

    John had to do the job (   ).

    Are they (   ) taking the whole responsibility?

    I plant the trees (   ).

6. What types of adjectives are the words in italics?

There were *four* birds on the balcony. (   )

Then a *fifth* one came along. (   )

Write two sentences using the same types of adjectives.

_____

_____

_____

_____

_____

_____